MW00788971

2025 Positive Affirmations Vision Board Clip Art Book: Empower Toolkit Series

Abyy Sparklewood

ISBN: 978-1-961634-63-3

Welcome to The Empower Toolkit Series: 2025 Positive Affirmations Vision Board & Clip Art Book! This edition is packed with over 400+ elements including vibrant images, phrases, quotes, and words designed for both men and women.

This book is your creative playground, filled with:
- Inspiring images
- Affirmations
- Empowering quotes

Designed to help you:
- Manifest your dreams
- Embrace your fullest potential

Whether you envision financial freedom, career success, or personal growth in 2025, this book is your companion on the journey to greatness.

Dive into pages brimming with:
- Vibrant clip art
- Symbols of wealth and abundance
- Uplifting pictures, phrases, and words

Let your imagination soar as you craft a vision board that reflects your unique aspirations and celebrates your beautiful, unstoppable self.

Get ready to:
- Turn your dreams into reality
- Empower yourself
- Prosper

Your journey to empowerment and prosperity starts here!

Quick Guide to Creating a Vision Board

Materials

- Poster board, magazines, printables, scissors, glue, markers, stickers, photos.

Steps

1. Define Goals: Focus on career, personal growth, health, relationships, etc.
2. Gather Materials: Set up your workspace with all needed items.
3. Find Inspiration: Cut out or print images and words that reflect your goals.
4. Arrange & Affix: Arrange on the board, then glue or pin items in place.
5. Add Personal Touches: Write goals, affirmations, or quotes.
6. Display: Place where you'll see it daily.
7. Review & Update: Adjust as your goals evolve.

A vision board brings your dreams to life—start today to stay focused and inspired!

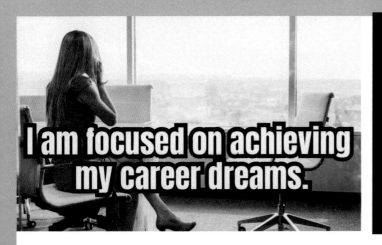

I am focused on achieving my career dreams.

Opportunities come my way because I am prepared.

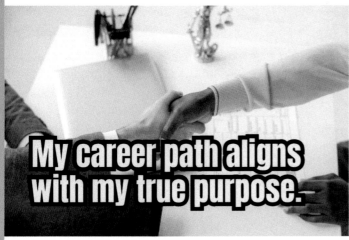

My career path aligns with my true purpose.

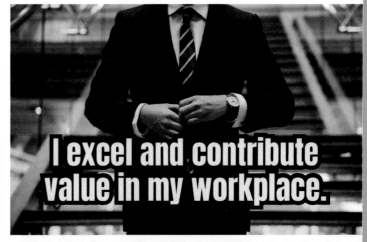

I excel and contribute value in my workplace.

DON'T QUIT!

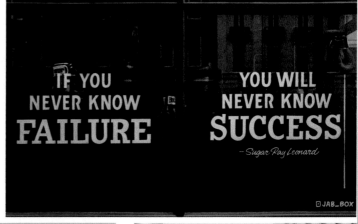

IF YOU NEVER KNOW FAILURE YOU WILL NEVER KNOW SUCCESS
— Sugar Ray Leonard

JAB_BOX

LADY BOSS

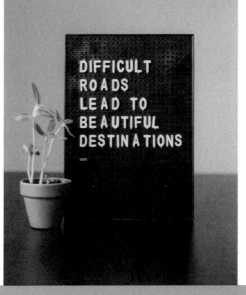

DIFFICULT ROADS LEAD TO BEAUTIFUL DESTINATIONS

Success is part of my daily journey.

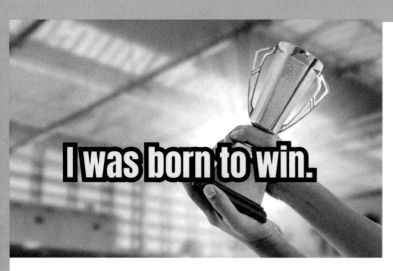

MAKE peace WITH YOUR PAST

You can Do it

YES YOU CAN

BELIEVE IN YOURSELF

BE THE GAME CHANGER

Good VIBES Only

ENJOY EVERY MOMENT

YOU ARE AMAZING!

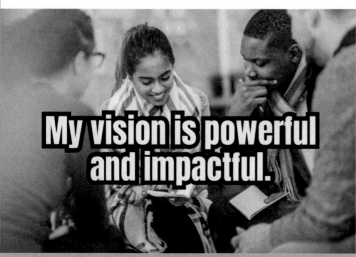

I am smart with my money.

Wealth flows to me abundantly.

I am successful financially.

My financial goals are within my reach.

My financial decisions are sound.

I invest wisely.

I am financially secure.

My future is bright and prosperous.

New Year's Resolutions

1. Quit smoking
2. Quit drinking
3. Lose weight
4. Join gym
5. Go back to school
6. Pay off debts
7. Find new job
8. Get organized
9. Volunteer
10. Find love ♥

My financial knowledge grows daily.

I manage my investments confidently.

My wealth multiplies with each investment.

Financial Education

I invest in myself and my future."

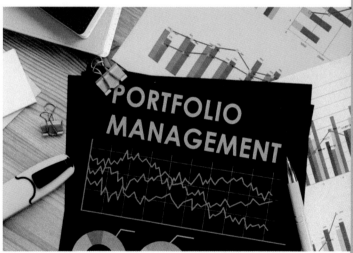

PORTFOLIO MANAGEMENT

CRYPTO

DIGITAL WALLET

I am worthy of love and respect.

"I am a supportive and loving partner.

I deserve a loving, nd suppotive Partner.

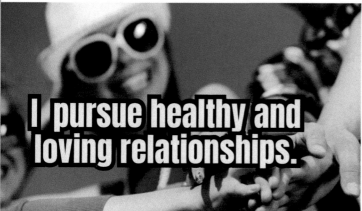

I pursue healthy and loving relationships.

Our love does not see color.

I deserve a devoted partner.

Love makes the world a better place.

Love binds us together.

I am grateful for meaningful friendships.

I love and cherish good friends.

True Love never fails.

friendship

smart

beautiful

kind

super

happy

see

the

good

my

kind

of

beautiful

you

are

super

only

happiness

Engagement & Wedding Dreams

I am ready for a lifetime of happiness.

I trust in the beauty of love's timing.

My future is filled with love and partnership.

I manifest my ideal partner.

Save the Date

Love and commitment bring joy to my life.

My life partner and I are connected deeply.

LOVE

Parenting Path

My family is rooted in love and respect.

I am patient and attentive in parenting.

I guide and support my children's dreams.

I am a nurturing and caring parent.

My little boy means the world to me.

Our family grows stronger every day.

I am grateful for my newborn.

I am a loyal and supportive friend.

I am surrounded by love.

Family & Friends

My family is my strength and my joy.

I cherish my family and friendships.

I create lasting memories with loved ones.

My relationships bring joy to my life.

Health is better than wealth

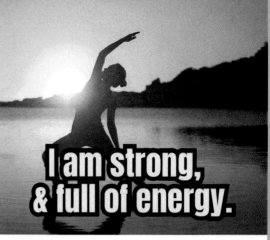
I am strong, & full of energy.

My wellness journey is balanced.

I love & care for my body daily.

My health is a priority.

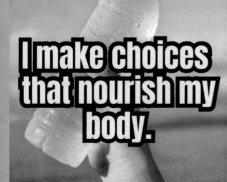
I make choices that nourish my body.

My body & mind are in harmony.

I am grateful for my good health.

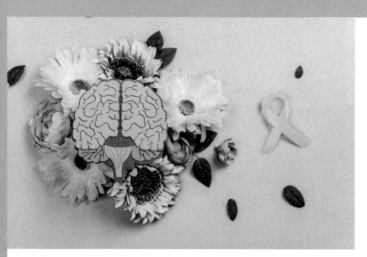

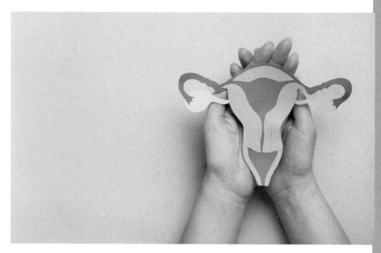

I am committed to my fitness journey

FITNESS TIPS

My body is strong, and resilient.

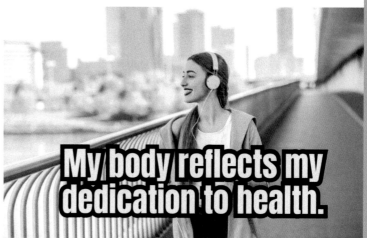

My body reflects my dedication to health.

Exercise rejuvenates my mind and body.

I love the feeling of being active and fit.

SET GOALS GET RESULTS

Taking care of myself brings me joy.

I nurture my mind, body, and soul.

My self-care rituals restore my energy.

I prioritize time for self-care and relaxation.

I love the feeling of being active and fit.

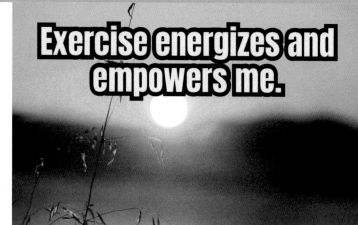

Exercise energizes and empowers me.

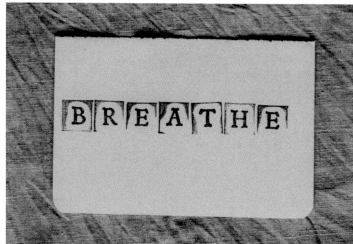

I celebrate every step of my fitness progress.

My body is strong and agile.

I dedicate time to things I love to do.

My hobbies enrich my life and spirit.

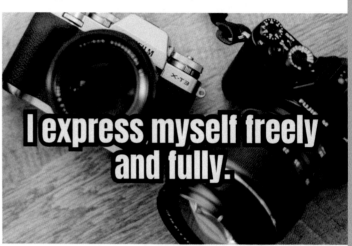

I express myself freely and fully.

I embrace my unique talents and passions.

My creativity brings joy and fulfillment.

DREAM BIG

DIY

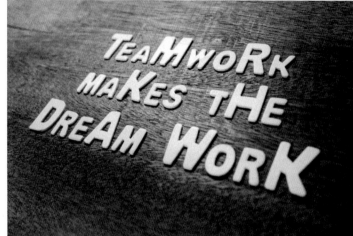

I am open to learning from new journeys.

Adventure is part of my life journey.

I embrace different cultures & experiences.

I am excited to explore new places.

Grateful for the chance to see the world.

HAVE
NO
FEAR
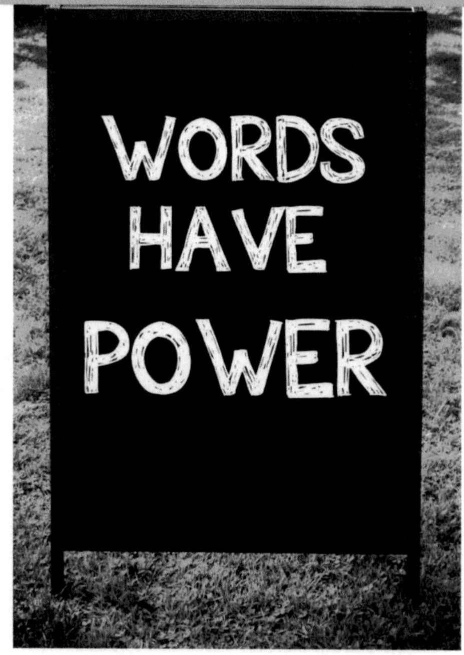
WORDS
HAVE
POWER

STRESS
FREE
ZONE

TODAY
IS THE
DAY

YOU'RE
ALMOST
THERE

DON'T
GIVE UP

A GOAL
WITHOUT
A PLAN IS
JUST A
WISH

CHOOSE
TO BE
HAPPY

LUCK
is not
a
STRATEGY

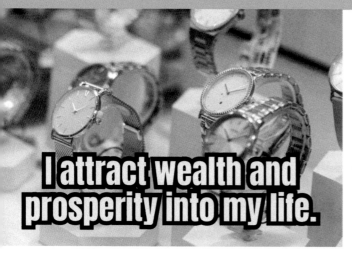

I attract wealth and prosperity into my life.

I am worthy of a life of abundance & luxury.

LUXURY lifestyle

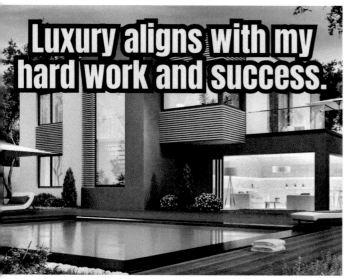

Luxury aligns with my hard work and success.

I embrace the beauty of luxury experiences.

I am grateful for the luxuries in my life.

I enjoy the finer things life has to offer.

Abundance	Ambition
Balance	Belief
Commitment	Creativity
Determination	Dream
Empower	Energy
Freedom	Faith
Growth	Gratitude
Healing	Hope
Inspiration	Imagination
Mindfulness	Joy

Pet Companions

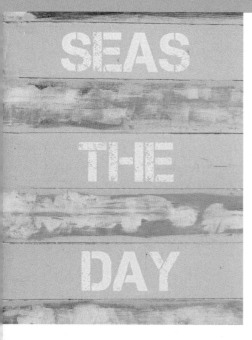

SEAS
THE
DAY

BE YOUR
BEAUTIFUL
SELF

GOOD
VIBES
ONLY

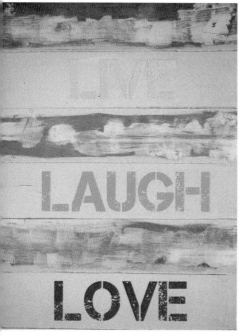

LIVE
LAUGH
LOVE

HAPPINESS
IS
A DAY AT THE
BEACH

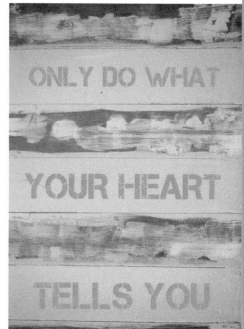

ONLY DO WHAT
YOUR HEART
TELLS YOU

FREE
BEER
TOMORROW

LIFE IS
BETTER AT
THE BEACH

LIFE
IS
BETTER
IN
FLIP FLOPS

777

Date _____

Pay to the
Order of _____ $ [_____]

_____ *Dollars*

⑆000000000⑆ 00000000000⑈ 0000

0001

Date _____ 20 ____

PAY TO THE
ORDER OF _____ $ [_____]

_____ DOLLARS 🔒 Security
Features
Details on
Back

For _____

⑆005552222 ⑉ ⑆005552222222⑈ 0001

0001

Date _____ 20 ____

PAY TO THE
ORDER OF _____ $ [_____]

_____ DOLLARS 🔒 Security
Details on
Back

For _____

⑆005552222 ⑉ ⑆005552222222⑈ 0001

0001

Date _____ 20 ____

PAY TO THE
ORDER OF _____ $ [_____]

_____ DOLLARS 🔒 Security
Features
Details on
Back

For _____

⑆005552222 ⑉ ⑆005552222222⑈ 0001

0001

Date _____ 20 ____

PAY TO THE
ORDER OF _____ $ [_____]

_____ DOLLARS 🔒 Security
Features
Details on
Back

For _____

⑆005552222 ⑉ ⑆005552222222⑈ 0001

1025

DATE _____

PAY TO THE
ORDER OF _____ $ [_____]

_____ DOLLARS 🔒 Security Features
Included
Details on Back

MEMO _____

⑆000000000⑆ ⑆000000000⑆ 1025

1025

DATE _____

PAY TO THE
ORDER OF _____ $ [_____]

_____ DOLLARS 🔒 Security Features
Included
Details on Back

MEMO _____

⑆000000000⑆ ⑆000000000⑆ 1025

1025

DATE _____

PAY TO THE
ORDER OF _____ $ [_____]

_____ DOLLARS 🔒 Security Features
Included
Details on Back

MEMO _____

⑆000000000⑆ ⑆000000000⑆ 1025

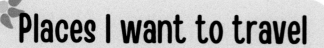 Places I want to travel

 New skills to learn

Personal Growth

Books to read

Restaurants to try

Financial Stability

Restaurants to try

Health and Fitness –

The 2025 Positive Affirmations Vision Board & Clip Art Book from The Empower Toolkit Series is your ultimate guide to manifesting dreams! Packed with over 400+ affirmation cards, phrases, and inspiring visuals, this book empowers you to embrace positivity, stay motivated, and take action toward a fulfilling, successful life. Make your dreams come alive—one empowering affirmation at a time!

Check out other books in The Empower Tool Kit series by scanning the QR code for more empowering resources!

Made in the USA
Las Vegas, NV
28 December 2024

15460635R00043